JOIN ...
OR ELSE!

Nick Toczek is a poet with three best-selling collections published by Macmillan Children's Books. They are *The Dragon Who Ate Our School, Dragons Everywhere* and *Never Stare At A Grizzly Bear*. He's also a professional story-teller, magician, puppeteer, journalist and stand-up comedian. *Join In . . . Or Else!* is his first anthology for Macmillan. For more information on Nick Toczek, check out his website at http://www.poems.fsnet.co.uk

David Parkins has illustrated numerous books, ranging from maths textbooks to *The Beano*. His picture books have been shortlisted for the Smarties Book Prize and the Kurt Maschler Award. He lives in Lincoln with his wife, three children and six cats.

JOIN IN OR ELSE!

Poems chosen by **Nick Toczek**

Illustrated by **David Parkins**

MACMILLAN CHILDREN'S BOOKS

First published 2000
by Macmillan Children's Books
a division of Macmillan Publishers Ltd
This edition produced 2002 for the
Book People Ltd,
Hall Wood Avenue,
Haydock, St Helens WA11 9UL

ISBN 0 330 48263 7

'Old Mrs Lazibones' by Gerda Mayer first published in *The Knockabout Show*
by Chatto and Windus 1978
'Sam, Sam, Quite Contrary' by Chrissie Gittins first published in *The Listening Station*
by Dagger Press 1998
'Poem About Love' by Fred Sedgwick first published by Tricky Sam! 1999
'The Cat from Down the Road' by Fred Sedgwick first published in
Pizza, Curry, Fish and Chips by Longmans 1994
'Ghosts' by Steve Turner first published in *The Day I Fell Down The Toilet* by Lion Publishing 1996
'This is the Key to the Castle' by Dave Calder first published in *Bamboozled* 1987
'Stuck Here For Ever' by Ian Souter first published in Poetry – Scholastic Collections
'Mr Punch' by John Mole first published in *Hot Air* by Hodder's Children's Books 1996
'I Wrote Me a Poem' by Bruce Barnes is based on an American children's song called
'I Bought Me a Cat.' Music © Boosey and Hawkes

Contents

Questions

What can you see
over the garden wall?

> It all depends on whether you're
> short or tall.

And when you're not looking
is what you saw still there?

> The pictures inside your head
> are everywhere.

What colour is the night
when you're fast asleep?

> No colour and every colour,
> dark and deep.

And what sound does a tree make
if no one hears it fall?

> Every sound you've ever heard,
> and no sound at all.

Tony Charles

March Time: Dance Time

One two three four, one two three four,
Left right, left right, stamp your feet.
One two three four, one two three four,
We go marching down the street.

One two three four, one two three four,
Swing your arms and breathe in deep.
One two three four, one two three four,
Up the hill however steep.

One two three four, one two three four,
Hold your head up, look your best.
One two three four, one two three four,
Soon be home and have a rest.

One two three four, one two three four,
Plod, plod . . . plod . . . plod. Feet like lead.
One two three four, one two three four,
All we want is to go to bed.

But –

One two three, one two three, one two three, one two three,
That's what we do when we skip.
One two three, one two three, one two three, one two three,
Leap in the air and don't slip.

One two three, one two three, one two three, one two three,
Tired? Never. Now we can fly.
One two three, one two three, one two three, one two three,
Up we go, ever so high.

One two three, one two three, one two three, one two three,
Out we go dancing to play.
One two three, one two three, one two three, one two three,
Iced-lolly-nice holiday.

One two three, one two three, one two three, one two
  three,
Mum's carried us up to bed.
One two three, one two three, one two three, one two
  three,
Dancing goes on in my head.

One two three, one two three, one two three, one two
  three,
Dreaming, we hop, skip, and leap.
One two three, one two three, one two three, one two
  three,
Mum whispers "Ssh! they're asleep."

Leo Aylen

I Wrote Me a Poem

I wrote me a poem, and the poem pleased me.
I told my poem to the big oak tree.
My poem went: "Fiddle-eye-dee".

I wrote me a sonnet, and the sonnet pleased me.
I told my sonnet to the big oak tree.
My sonnet went: "Ooh, love!" *(action: do a loud kiss)*
My poem went: "Fiddle-eye-dee".

I wrote me an ode, and the ode pleased me.
I told my ode to the big oak tree.
My ode went: "Lah . . . dah".
My sonnet went: "Oooh, love!" (loud kiss)
My poem went: "Fiddle-eye-dee".

I wrote me an epic, and the epic pleased me.
I told my epic to the big oak tree.
My epic went: "Too long, much too long". *(stretch out arms)*
My ode went: "Lah . . . dah".
My sonnet went: "Oooh, love!" (loud kiss)
My poem went: "Fiddle-eye-dee".

I wrote me a verse, and the verse pleased me.
I told my verse to the big oak tree.
My verse went "Tickety-boo, tickety-boo".
My epic went: "Too long, much too long". (stretch out arms)
My ode went: "Lah . . . dah".
My sonnet went: "Oooh, love!" (loud kiss)
My poem went: "Fiddle-eye-dee".

I wrote me a haiku and the haiku pleased me.
I told my haiku to the big oak tree.
My haiku went: "Slooooow thought".
My verse went "Tickety-boo, tickety-boo".
My epic went: "Too long, much too long". (stretch out arms)
My ode went: "Lah ... dah".
My sonnet went: "Oooh, love!" (loud kiss)
My poem went: "Fiddle-eye-dee".

I wrote me a rhyme and the rhyme pleased me.
I told my rhyme to the big oak tree.
My rhyme went: "Sky high". *(stretch arms upwards)*
My haiku went: "Slooooow thought".
My verse went "Tickety-boo, tickety-boo".
My epic went: "Too long, much too long". (stretch out arms)
My ode went: "Lah ... dah".
My sonnet went: "Oooh, love!" (loud kiss)
My poem went: "Fiddle-eye-dee".

I wrote me a limerick and the limerick pleased me.
I told my limerick to the big oak tree.
My limerick went: "Silly-billy". *(wag finger)*
My rhyme went: "Sky high". (stretch arms upwards)
My haiku went: "Slooooow thought".
My verse went "Tickety-boo, tickety-boo".
My epic went: "Too long, much too long". (stretch out arms)
My ode went: "Lah ... dah".
My sonnet went: "Oooh, love!" (loud kiss)
My poem went: "Fiddle-eye-dee".

I wrote me a song and the song pleased me.
I told my song to the big oak tree.
My song went: "Tree Shanty".
My limerick went: "Silly-billy". (wag finger)
My rhyme went: "Sky high". (stretch arms upwards)
My haiku went: "Slooooow thought".
My verse went "Tickety-boo, tickety-boo".
My epic went: "Too long, much too long". (stretch out arms)
My ode went: "Lah ... dah".
My sonnet went: "Oooh, love!" (loud kiss)
My poem went: "Fiddle-eye-dee".

I wrote me some words and the words pleased me.
I told my words to the big oak tree.
My words went: "Jibber-jabber".
My song went: "Tree Shanty".
My limerick went: "Silly-billy". (wag finger)
My rhyme went: "Sky high". (stretch arms upwards)
My haiku went: "Slooooow thought".
My verse went "Tickety-boo, tickety-boo".
My epic went: "Too long, much too long". (stretch out arms)
My ode went: "Lah ... dah".
My sonnet went: "Oooh, love!" (loud kiss)
My poem went: "Fiddle-eye-dee".

Bruce Barnes

Saturday Evening

From Dundee to Dover
The games are all over
And those who have lost
Will be counting the cost . . .

I know it'll vex 'em
In Rochdale and Wrexham.
At Clydebank and Clyde
They'll have cried and have cried.
They'll be glumly pathetic
At Charlton Athletic,
But moodily manly
At Accrington Stanley.

Cos nobody likes to lose.
They stand there and stare at their shoes.
They're gobsmacked and gutted
Like they've been head-butted.
Life's not worth a carrot.
They're sick as a parrot
And struggle to cope with the news.

At Manchester City
They're full of self-pity.
At Port Vale they're pale,
At Alloa, sallower,
Sullen in Fulham,
Morose at Montrose,
And Bradford and Burnley
Just sulk taciturnly.

Cos nobody likes to lose.
They stand there and stare at their shoes.
They're gobsmacked and gutted
Like they've been head-butted.
Life's not worth a carrot.
They're sick as a parrot
And struggle to cope with the news.

And down Grimsby Town
Oh, how grimly they frown!
And Partick and Chelsea
Grow sick and unhealthy,
While at Aston Villa
They're very much iller,
And it's really killing 'em
In Millwall and Gillingham.

Cos nobody likes to lose.
They stand there and stare at their shoes.
They're gobsmacked and gutted
Like they've been head-butted.
Life's not worth a carrot.
They're sick as a parrot
And struggle to cope with the news.

In Barnsley and Barnet
They spit and say: "Darn it!"
At Preston North End
Now they're nobody's friend.
And down Crystal Palace
They bristle with malice,
While Reading and Rangers
Start beating up strangers.

Cos nobody likes to lose.
They stand there and stare at their shoes.
They're gobsmacked and gutted.
Like they've been head-butted.
Life's not worth a carrot.
They're sick as a parrot
And struggle to cope with the news.

They're not very merry
In Blackburn and Bury.
They're choking in Woking
Where no one is joking.
There's an air of despair
In the air over Ayr,
And the black cloud's a big 'un
That hangs over Wigan.

Cos nobody likes to lose.
They stand there and stare at their shoes.
They're gobsmacked and gutted.
Like they've been head-butted.
Life's not worth a carrot.
They're sick as a parrot
And struggle to cope with the news.

Nick Toczek

Monkey Motto

I leap through the trees.
I drop to the ground.
That's what I do –
Monkey around.

I pounce on my tail.
I bounce and I bound.
That's what I do –
Monkey around.

I spit out the pips
Of fruit I have found.
That's what I do –
Monkey around.

I hear my own hoots.
I shriek at the sound.
That's what I do –
Monkey around.

Want to have fun
That won't cost a pound
Here's what you do –
Monkey around.

Clare Bevan

(Note: A good excuse for actions and jungle noises.)

Boots

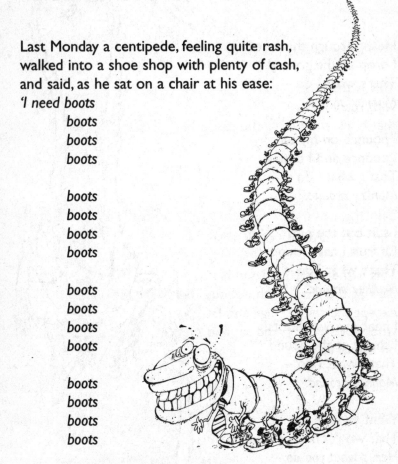

Last Monday a centipede, feeling quite rash,
walked into a shoe shop with plenty of cash,
and said, as he sat on a chair at his ease:
'I need boots
> *boots*
> *boots*
> *boots*

> *boots*
> *boots*
> *boots*
> *boots*

> *boots*
> *boots*
> *boots*
> *boots*

> *boots*
> *boots*
> *boots*
> *boots*

boots, if you please.'

Barry Buckingham

who wishes to point out that, in spite of the name, centipedes do not
have a hundred legs. If they did, this poem would go on and on and on
and on and on and ...

This is the Key to the Castle

This is the key to the castle

This is the box
with rusty locks
that holds the key to the castle

This is the spider, huge and fat,
who wove its web and sat and sat
on top of the box
with rusty locks
that holds the key to the castle

This is the cellar, cold and bare,
dark as the grave, with nobody there
except the spider, huge and fat,
who wove its web and sat and sat
on top of the box
with rusty locks
that holds the key to the castle

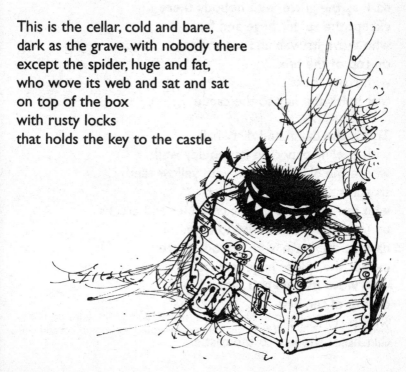

This is the stair that crumbles and creaks
where every small step moans and squeaks
that leads to the cellar, cold and bare,
dark as the grave, with nobody there
except the spider, huge and fat,
who wove its web and sat and sat
on top of the box
with rusty locks
that holds the key to the castle

This is the rat with yellow teeth,
sharp as sorrow, long as grief,
who ran up the stair that crumbles and creaks
where every small step moans and squeaks
up from the cellar, cold and bare,
dark as the grave, with nobody there
except the spider, huge and fat,
who wove its web and sat and sat
on top of the box
with rusty locks
that holds the key to the castle

This is the damp and dirty hall
with peeling paper on its mouldy wall
where the black rat runs with yellow teeth
sharp as sorrow, long as grief,
who ran up the stair that crumbles and creaks
up from the cellar, cold and bare,
dark as the grave, with nobody there
except the spider, huge and fat,
who wove its web and sat and sat
on top of the box
with rusty locks
that holds the key to the castle

This is the ghost with rattling bones,
carrying his head, whose horrible groans
fill the damp and dirty hall
with peeling paper on its mouldy wall
where the black rat runs with yellow teeth
sharp as sorrow, long as grief,
who ran up the stair that crumbles and creaks
up from the cellar, cold and bare,
dark as the grave, with nobody there
except the spider, huge and fat,
who wove its web and sat and sat
on top of the box
with rusty locks
that holds the key to the castle

This is the child who came in to play
on a rainy, windy, nasty day

and said BOO! to the ghost who groaned in the hall
and SCAT! to the rat by the mouldy wall
and went down the creaking crumbling stair
into the cellar, cold and bare,
and laughed at the spider, huge and fat,
and brushed off the web where it sat and sat
and opened the box
with rusty locks
and took the key to the castle.

Dave Calder

Cupboard Love

Apple pie and cider,
Who's afraid of spiders?
Sally caught the old grey mare,
But found she couldn't ride her.
She's got ribbons in her hair
Hanging down beside her.
Apple pie and cider
Who's afraid of spiders?

Voice 1:	My spider's got nine legs,
Voice 2:	He lives in my pocket,
Voice 3:	He drinks cups of coffee,
Voice 4:	He eats purple parrots with mustard and toffee
Voice 5:	And washing lines and clothes pegs
Voice 6:	And butter beans and kedgeree,
Voice 7:	And basketballs and cricket bats.
Voice 8:	On summer evenings after tea, He goes outside and hunts for cats.

Apple pie and cider,
Who's afraid of spiders?
Sally caught the old grey mare,
But found she couldn't ride her.
She's got ribbons in her hair
Hanging down beside her.
Apple pie and cider
Who's afraid of spiders?

Tony Charles

Fish and Chips on Friday

They're eating pasta in Nebraska,
Tortillas in Dundee,
But it's Friday,
So at our house
It's fish and chips for tea.

Ratatouille in St Louis,
Faggots in Bahrain,
But it's Friday,
So at our house
It's fish and chips again.

Risotto in Somoto,
Crepe Suzette in Mors,
But it's Friday,
So at our house
It's fish and chips – of course.

John Coldwell

The Dragon Who Ate Our School

The day the dragon came to call
she ate the gate, the playground wall
and, slate by slate, the roof and all,
the staffroom, gym, and entrance hall.
And every classroom, big or small.

So ...
She's undeniably great.
She's absolutely cool,
the dragon who ate
the dragon who ate
the dragon who ate our school.

Pupils panicked. Teachers ran.
She flew at them with wide wingspan.
She slew a few and then began
to chew through the lollipop man,
two parked cars and a transit van.

Wow ... !
She's undeniably great.
She's absolutely cool,
the dragon who ate
the dragon who ate
the dragon who ate our school.

She bit off the head of the head.
She said she was sad he was dead.
He bled and he bled and he bled.
And as she fed, her chin went red
and then she swallowed the cycle shed.

Oh ...
She's undeniably great.
She's absolutely cool,
the dragon who ate
the dragon who ate
the dragon who ate our school.

It's thanks to her that we've been freed.
We needn't write. We needn't read.
Me and my mates are all agreed,
we're very pleased with her indeed.
So clear the way, let her proceed.

Cos ...
She's undeniably great.
She's absolutely cool,
the dragon who ate
the dragon who ate
the dragon who ate our school.

There was some stuff she couldn't eat.
A monster forced to face defeat,
she spat it out along the street –
the dinner ladies' veg and meat
and that pink muck they serve for sweet.

But ...
She's undeniably great.
She's absolutely cool,
the dragon who ate
the dragon who ate
the dragon who ate our school.

Nick Toczek

Clap-Clap Clappity Clap

Angela, Angela, dance with me,
Over the water and over the sea.
                Clap-clap, clappity clap.

Bridget, Bridget, laugh with me,
Over the water and over the sea.
                Clap-clap, clappity clap.

Caroline, Caroline, sing with me,
Over the water and over the sea.
                Clap-clap, clappity clap.

Deborah, Deborah, talk with me,
Over the water and over the sea.
                Clap-clap, clappity clap.

Erica, Erica, write to me,
Over the water and over the sea.
                Clap-clap, clappity clap.

Fiona, Fiona, walk with me,
Over the water and over the sea.
                Clap-clap, clappity clap.

Gerri, Gerri, play with me,
Over the water and over the sea.
                Clap-clap, clappity clap.

Hannah, Hannah, read with me,
Over the water and over the sea.
Clap-clap, clappity clap.

Isobel, Isobel, hop with me,
Over the water and over the sea.
   Clap-clap, clappity clap.

Jackie, Jackie, stroll with me,
Over the water and over the sea.
   Clap-clap, clappity clap.

  (And so on, while there are enough names)

Children all, wherever you may be,
Over the water and over the sea.
   Clap-clap, clappity clap.

Come in a circle, clap with me,
Over the water and over the sea.
   Clap-clap, clappity clap.

(Note: This is a circular action/clapping song. Any names and actions can be included, to suit the group.)

Jennifer Curry

Ouch!

A painful way to sit is with a slouch
> *Ouch!*
> *Ouch!*

Or on a spring that's sticking from a couch
> *Ouch!*
> *Ouch!*

A painful way to walk is with a crouch
> *Ouch!*
> *Ouch!*

And painful, isn't it, when people grouch
> *Ouch!*
> *Ouch!*

Peter Waddell

(Note: Everyone acts out the poem and says the Ouches!)

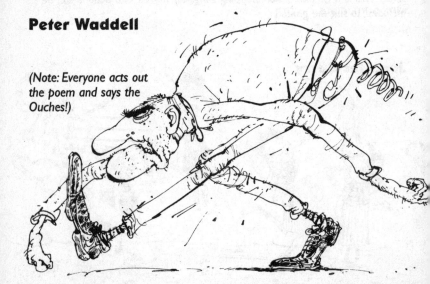

Sam, Sam, Quite Contrary

Sam, Sam, quite contrary
bought a budgie,
wanted a canary.

Sam, Sam, quite contrary
kissed Suzannah,
meant to kiss Mary

Sam, Sam, quite contrary
dressed as a pirate,
playing a fairy.

Sam, Sam, quite contrary
eats dark chocolate,
says he likes dairy.

Sam, Sam, quite contrary
shaved his head,
to make it hairy.

Chrissie Gittins

Work Song

Your body's good to you
    Go body, go
pumps around your blood for you
    Go body, go
goes through puddles and mud for you
    Go body, go
without it – what would you do?
    Go body, go

Yes, go body, go!

On your hands you can depend
    Go body, go
the ones you wave to all your friends
    Go body, go
if I didn't have mine I couldn't count to ten
    Go body, go
how else do your arms know where to end?
    Go body, go

Yes, go body, go!

Now legs they really are great
    Go body, go
on skateboards, stilts or roller skates
    Go body, go
wish I was a spider so I could have eight!
    Go body, go
Without legs – how you gonna stand up straight?
    Go body, go

Yes, go body, go!

Now your bottom's gotta be your number one
       Go body, go
it's the bit you hang your Levi's on
       Go body, go
make those funny noises from
       Go body, go
without one – what d'you sit upon?
       Go body, go

Yes, go body, go!

Now your feet you treat 'em gently
       Go body, go
cos they're gonna get trodden on plenty
       Go body, go
they fill your socks up when they're empty
       Go body, go
how else can you dance the Top 20?
       Go body, go

Yes, go body, go!

C'mon give your head three cheers
       Go body, go
full right up with bright ideas
       Go body, go
I've had mine for years and years
       Go body, go
without one – where'd'you keep your ears?
       Go body, go

Yes, go body, go!

Now your body is the one you gotta stay with
>   *Go body, go*
it's the one you'll spend each day with
>   *Go body, go*
it's the one you'll grow old and grey with
>   *Go body, go*
without it – who you gonna play with?
>   *Go body, go*

>   *So go body, go!*
>   *Yes, go body, go!*
>   *I said, go body, go!*

David Horner

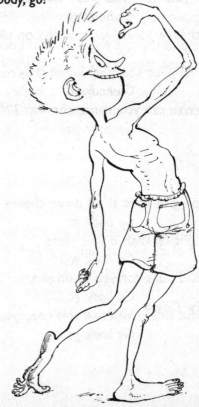

Hear Here

1. The stallion neighed, and thundered round the course.
He neighed until his throat was sore: *hoarse horse*

2. He won his spurs, he fought for what was right
But never in the daylight hours: *night knight*

3. At first the stone was timid. It grew older
And learned to be courageous: *bolder boulder*

4. Poor Bruin feels the chilly winter air
Because he's losing all his fur: *bare bear*

5. Check your spelling, try with all your might
To be grammatical and clear: *write right*

6. The punishment was fair. He'd been a swine
And he deserved to pay for it: *fine fine*

7. Yes, I insulted her, as well I might.
I wouldn't call the insult gross: *slight slight*

8. The meeting drags. Directors can't afford
To fall asleep. They must endure: *bored board*

9. The publican's ejected him. It's hard.
The poet cannot buy a pint: *barred bard*

10. Be quiet, pay attention, lend an ear.
This is a place for listening: *hear here*

Wendy Cope

Caterpillar (with hand actions)

Caterpillar, caterpillar,
Lots of feet.

(fingers crawl over surface: desktop or knees)

Caterpillar, caterpillar,
Lots to eat.

(fingers and thumbs form jaws and chew)

Caterpillar, caterpillar,
Spin, spin, spin.

(fingers of each hand intertwine, wriggling rapidly)

Caterpillar, chrysalis,
Change within.

(hands mesh with fingers tucked inside, still wriggling)

Chrysalis, chrysalis,
Long, dark night.

(thumbs hook into each other, fingers still wriggling)

Chrysalis, butterfly,
Take to flight.

(hands spread flat becoming flapping wings, thumbs still hooked together)

Ian Larmont

I've Never Seen
(after John Rice)

I've never seen a fridge climb a tree.
I've never seen a dog as small as a bee.
I've never seen a lamp-post shake my hand.
I've never seen a tiger play in a band.

I've never seen a pigeon smoke a pipe.
I've never seen an elephant learn to type.
I've never seen a television dance a jig.
I've never seen a pillar-box swallow a pig.

I've never seen a feather that weighed a ton.
I've never seen an igloo built on the sun.
I've never seen a mountain wear a hat.
I've never seen a caterpillar catapult a cat.

Have you?

Charles Thomson

Christine Crump

First voice: Christine Crump is crunching crisps.
Second voice: Cheese and onion, cheese and onion.
First voice: Christine Crump has crunched them.

First voice: Christine Crump is crunching crisps.
Third voice: Smoky bacon, smoky bacon,
Second voice: Cheese and onion, cheese and onion.
First voice: Christine Crump has crunched them.

First voice: Christine Crump is crunching crisps.
Fourth voice: Ready salted, ready salted,
Third voice: Smoky bacon, smoky bacon,
Second voice: Cheese and onion, cheese and onion.
First voice: Christine Crump has crunched them.

First voice: Christine Crump is crunching crisps.
Fifth voice: Curry flavour, curry flavour,
Fourth voice: Ready salted, ready salted,
Third voice: Smoky bacon, smoky bacon,
Second voice: Cheese and onion, cheese and onion.
First voice: Christine Crump has crunched them.

First voice: Christine Crump is crunching crisps.
Sixth voice: Salt and vinegar, salt and vinegar,
Fifth voice: Curry flavour, curry flavour,
Fourth voice: Ready salted, ready salted,
Third voice: Smoky bacon, smoky bacon,
Second voice: Cheese and onion, cheese and onion.
First voice: Christine Crump has crunched them.

First voice: Christine Crump is feeling sick . . .
Altogether: Poor old Christine, pool old Christine,
First voice: She has indigestion.

Colin West

Things To Cheer And Boo

They're pulling the old school down	*Hurrah!*
And building a new one in its place	*Boo!*
There'll only be one teacher.	*Hurrah!*
One teacher for every six pupils.	*Boo!*
They won't expect pupils to work hard.	*Hurrah!*
They'll expect them to work very hard.	*Boo!*
You won't be sent out at break when it's raining.	*Hurrah!*
Because there won't be any break.	*Boo!*
There'll be no end of year exams.	*Hurrah!*
There'll be exams every week.	*Boo!*
You'll be sent home early on Fridays.	*Hurrah!*
And kept to midnight on the other days.	*Boo!*
The summer holidays start on July 1st	*Hurrah!*
And end on July 2nd.	*Boo!*
They're pulling the old school down	*Hurrah!*
And building a new one in its place.	*Boo!*

John Coldwell

I'm Proud To Be

I'm proud to be what I am
I'm proud to be what I am

Could be English
Or from the Caribbean
   Could be Asian
   Or an African
   Could be fat or thin
   Or very small
   4 feet two
Or six feet tall

I'm proud to be what I am
I'm proud to be what I am

Could be black or white
Or yellow or brown
   Living in the poorer
   Side of town
   Might be slick
   Might be cool
Might not break laws
Might not break rules

I'm proud to be what I am
I'm proud to be what I am

May not have
   Designer gear
May not have
   Great things to wear
May not have
   A new CD
May not have
    Your own TV.

I'm proud to be what I am
I'm proud to be what I am

It ain't what yer got
   It's who yer are
   Will take yer places
   'N' take yer far
Respect yer uncle, yer auntie
   Yer sister yer brother
   Yer cousin, yer niece
   Yer father yer mother

I'm proud to be what I am
I'm proud to be what I am

We're all the world's people
One family
   And that includes you
   And that includes me
   You are what you are
   You should be proud

So stand up straight
   And shout out loud

I'm proud to be what I am
I'm proud to be what I am

Martin Glynn

The Conversation

Said the worm to the bird:
Is it cold up there
In the huge, great, shivery
Spacious air?
I've heard that the wind
When it blows, can blow
Somewhere to nowhere . . .
Is it so?
Somewhere to nowhere . . .
Is it so?

Said the bird to the worm:
I suppose you stay
in a tunnel of darkness
Night and day,
Squiggling, wriggling,
Smooth and pink.
It must be monotonous,
I should think?
It must be monotonous,
I should think?

Said the worm to the bird:
Is it nice to fly
From sky to tree
And from tree to sky?
Are the sun and the moon
And the stars as near
As the stones and the seed

To me, down here?
As the stones and the seed
To me, down here?

Said the bird to the worm:
What a tail you've got!
Do you find it gets
In the way a lot?
And wouldn't it be
A peculiar thing
If birds should squiggle
And worms could sing!
If birds should squiggle
And worms could sing!

Jean Kenward

(Note: This is a poem for three voices, that of bird, worm and a narrator who says the first line of each stanza. The audience joins in by repeating the last two lines. The poet suggests possible use of costume, mime and musical accompaniment).

Mr Punch

Did he have friends
When he was a kid?
Oh no he didn't.
Oh yes he did.

Was he ever upset
When his mum got so cross?
Oh no he wasn't.
Oh yes he was.

Had he frightened his sister
And laughed at his dad?
Oh no he hadn't.
Oh yes he had.

Should he learn manners
And try to be good?
Oh no he shouldn't.
Oh yes he should.

Does he go calling
Policemen 'The Fuzz'?
Oh no he doesn't.
Oh yes he does.

When he is told to
Will he sit still?
Oh no he won't.
Oh yes he will.

Has he made up with Judy
Or turned down his jazz?
Oh no he hasn't.
Oh yes he has.

If he tried to explain
Would he be understood?
Oh no he wouldn't.
Oh yes he would.

Or must he stay always
A man we can't trust?
Oh no he mustn't.
Oh yes he must.

John Mole

Poem About Love

Rebecca fancies Robert.
> Robert dreams of Dee.
Dee is crazy about Dave
> *But Dave just wants his tea.*

Mary Jane McMullen loves
> A boy who's in Year Eight –
He's asked Mary's sister
> Sally for a date
> *But Dave just wants his tea.*

Larry's girl is Anne-Louise
> (Or so Larry has said)
But Anne-Louise kissed Lenny twice
> Behind the cricket shed
> *But Dave just wants his tea.*

Farida dotes on Darren,
> Darren's darling's Jen.
Jen kissed Jonathan and Jack
> And James – then Jack again
> *But Dave just wants his tea.*

Anna's beau is Andrew.
> Andrew can't stand her
While Maggie, Meg and Margaret
> Only fancy Sir
> *But Dave just wants his tea.*

Freda fancies Fariq,
    Fariq's girl is Gus.
The vicar says, surprisingly,
    God loves the lot of us
    But Dave just wants his tea.

Fred Sedgwick

It Makes Dad Mad

Let's ransack the toy box,
Cos it makes Dad mad.
Let's squeeze jelly in our socks,
Cos it makes Dad mad.
Let's wrestle in the flower beds,
And pour the compost on our heads;
Let's lock the dog in the garden shed,
Cos it makes Dad mad.

Let's spread toothpaste on the telly,
Cos it makes Dad mad.
Let's pour rhubarb in our wellies,
Cos it makes Dad mad.
Let's burst a bag of flour,
And put frogspawn in the shower;
Let's just scream for half an hour,
Cos it makes Dad mad.

Let's stamp in muddy puddles,
Cos it makes Dad mad.
Let's fill the bathroom up with bubbles,
Cos it makes Dad mad.
Let's tip treacle on the cat,
And chase it with a cricket bat;
Let's cut up the front door mat,
Cos it makes Dad mad.

Dad's asleep, don't wake him up.
The room's a mess, but we'll scrape it up.
He'll want some tea, so we'll make a cup.
Quiet – you can hear him snore,
He won't mind the sugar on the floor,
And all the milk spilt up on the wall ...
Watch the carpet – don't you fall!
What did you go and do that for?
COS IT MAKES DAD MAD!!

Dave Ward

Stuck Here For Ever!

1st gear,
    2nd gear,
        3rd gear – never!
Are we to be stuck in this traffic jam for ever?

With:

Cars slowing and traffic growing,
Bumpers nudging, hardly budging.
Stop – start, stop – start, no overtaking!
Stop – start, stop – start, continual breaking!

1st gear,
    2nd gear,
        3rd gear – never!
Are we to be stuck in this traffic jam for ever?

With:

Babies crying and mothers sighing,
Drivers glaring and horns blaring.
Honk! Honk! Honk! Peep! Peep! Peep!
Cars, cars, cars like sheep, sheep, sheep!

1st gear,
        2nd gear,
                3rd gear – never!
Are we to be stuck in this traffic jam for ever?

With:

Engines turning and fumes burning,
Petrol oxidising and pollution rising.
Smoke! Smoke! Smoke! Choke! Choke! Choke!
A solution to pollution; a master stroke!

1st hour
        2nd hour,
                3rd hour's gone.
I'll be another year older before we move on!

Ian Souter

Old Mrs Lazibones

Old Mrs Lazibones
And her dirty daughter
Never used soap
And never used water.

> *Higgledy piggledy cowpat*
> *What d'you think of that?*

Daisies from their fingernails,
Birds' nests in their hair-O,
Dandelions from their ears –
What a dirty pair-O!

> *Higgledy piggledy cowpat*
> *What d'you think of that?*

Came a prince who sought a bride,
Riding past their doorstep,
Quick, said Mrs Lazibones,
Girl, under the watertap.

> *Higgledy piggledy cowpat*
> *What d'you think of that?*

Washed her up and washed her down,
Then she washed her sideways,
But the prince was far, far away,
He'd ridden off on the highways.

> *Higgledy piggledy cowpat*
> *What d'you think of that?*

Gerda Mayer

Great-Gran is Manic on her Motorbike

Shout out loud, say what you like
Great-Gran is manic on her motorbike.

Last week her helmet touched the stars
when she zoomed over thirty cars
she didn't quibble, didn't fuss
when they added a double-decker bus.

Shout out loud, say what you like
Great-Gran is manic on her motorbike.

She's a headline-hunting, bike-stunting
wacky-wild-one-woman-show
she revs and roars to wild applause
there is no place her bike won't go
she gives them shivers jumping rivers
and balancing across high wires
with a cheer she changes gear
flies her bike through blazing tyres.

Shout out loud, say what you like
Great-Gran is manic on her motorbike.

She told me when she quits bike-riding
she's going to take up paragliding
I'll always be her greatest fan
my dazzling, daredevil, manic Great-Gran!

Shout out loud, say what you like
Great-Gran is manic on her motorbike.

David Harmer

The Cat from Down the Road

I am the cat from down the road.

I am the cat from down the road.
(neighbours call me James).

I am the cat from down the road.
(neighbours call me James)
and I've adopted all of you
from twenty-one to eighty-two
to give me milk and comfort too.

I am the cat from down the road.
(neighbours call me James)
and I've adopted all of you
from twenty-one to eighty-two
to give me milk and comfort too.
Stroke me. Call me pleasant names.

I am the cat from down the road.
(neighbours call me James)
and I've adopted all of you
from twenty-one to eighty-two
to give me milk and comfort too.
Stroke me. Call me pleasant names.
When your front door opens, I'm
always inside in record time.

I am the cat from down the road.
(neighbours call me James)
and I've adopted all of you
from twenty-one to eighty-two
to give me milk and comfort too.
Stroke me. Call me pleasant names.
When your front door opens, I'm
always inside in record time.
I mew and moan till the saucer comes.

I am the cat from down the road.
(neighbours call me James)
and I've adopted all of you
from twenty-one to eighty-two
to give me milk and comfort too.
Stroke me. Call me pleasant names.
When your front door opens, I'm
always inside in record time.
I mew and moan till the saucer comes.
I lap and stretch till the saucer comes.

I am the cat from down the road.
(neighbours call me James).

Fred Sedgwick

Ghosts

I'd like to be a ghost, I would.
To be a ghost is cool.
For ghosts don't have to go to work
And ghosts don't go to school.

A ghost can stay up late at night
(In fact they always do).
And ghosts get rooms all to themselves
By simply shouting: *"whooooooooooooooooo!"*

Steve Turner